L-I-T *Guide*
Literature In Teaching

The Summer
of the Swans
Betsy Byars

The Summer of the Swans
Written by Betsy Byars

STORY SUMMARY

This is the story of Sara and her two siblings, Wanda and Charlie. Their mother died several years ago, and their father sent them to live with their aunt. The four live in a small town in West Virginia. Sara feels somewhat deserted by their father, who rarely comes to visit.

Fourteen-year-old Sara is having a terrible summer! She is suffering from the awkwardness and mood swings of adolescence. She desperately seeks the approval of her peers and often feels that she is living in the shadow of her older, more attractive sister. Sara feels that Wanda is self-absorbed and overly concerned about her dating and social life; nevertheless, Wanda is sympathetic to Sara and offers companionship and advice when Sara is upset. Things are somewhat complicated by the fact that Charlie, their younger brother, is mentally retarded.

Sara takes Charlie to a nearby lake to see the swans, which recently arrived. Charlie is fascinated and does not want to leave. That night Charlie thinks about the swans and sets out to find them on his own. Although he has been told never to leave the yard alone, he somehow thinks this is different.

Charlie gets lost almost immediately and he is overcome with fear. Sara checks the lake but cannot find him, and Aunt Willie has no choice but to call the police. The police send out a search party, and the neighbors join in the effort. Sara, too, continues her search.

While searching for Charlie, Sara is joined by her classmate Joe Melby. Sara reluctantly accepts his help, for she blames him for teasing Charlie and taking his watch. She soon comes to realize, however, that she had misjudged him. With Joe's help, Sara finds Charlie. Although he is very upset, he is safe and sound.

Sara learns a lot about herself and about growing up from this experience. The rest of the summer looks a lot brighter!

Meet the Author
Betsy (Cromer) Byars

"There is no activity in my life which has brought me more pleasure than my writing," declared the award-winning author during a recent interview. Although she read a great deal as a child growing up in Charlotte, North Carolina, Betsy did not write very much. She explained, "I thought writers must have a boring life, sitting in a room alone and typing." She seemed to be mathematically inclined, and her parents hoped she would become a successful mathematician.

Betsy did begin her college career at Furman University as a math major, but she quickly realized that she was better suited to English. She earned her degree in English from Queens College in 1950. After her marriage to Edward Ford Byars and the birth of their first two children, Betsy began writing for magazines. "I had never thought of writing until my husband became a graduate student and I found myself with long hours to fill," she explained. The author's humorous articles were published by the *Saturday Evening Post* and *Look Magazine.* Her first foray into the world of children's literature began in the early 1960's. *Clementine* was published in 1962.

Byars often used familiar subjects and experiences as the basis for her novels. She told how she got her ideas: "I got ideas from things that happened around me—in newspaper articles, in things my children told me happen in their schools, in magazine articles." Marc Hammerman, the tough character in *The Eighteenth Emergency,* reminded her of a bully she had known in the third grade. The author's participation in a local program for mentally retarded children served as the inspiration for *The Summer of the Swans.* This book, winner of the Newbery Award, was published in 1971. It was adapted as an ABC After-School Special in 1974.

Other award-winning books by Byars include *The House of Wings, The Midnight Fox, The Pinballs, The TV Kid,* and *Trouble River.* Byars often based her writing on troubled children and their sometimes difficult family relationships.

Byars enjoys outdoor living and flying with her husband in his glider. She continues to delight her young readers with her sympathetic and realistic stories. Her latest books are *Seven Treasure Hunts* and *Wanted—Mud Blossom.*

Pre-Reading Information
The Whistling Swan

There are seven different types of swans in the world. Swans have long, graceful necks and are closely related to geese and ducks. Swans eat worms, shellfish, and water plants.

Only one species is native to North America: the whistling swan. Also known as the tundra swan, this species is very large—about 36 inches—and, except for a yellow spot between the nostrils and the eyes, its body is all white or very pale yellow. Its legs, feet, and bill are black.

The whistling swan nests around the Arctic Circle and in the winter migrates to the coastal regions of the United States. Between October and April, V-shaped flocks of whistling swans are seen and heard as they migrate. Some have been observed flying at forty to fifty miles per hour! In the east, flocks reach as far south as South Carolina. They can be recognized by their distinguishing muffled call.

The diet of the whistling swan consists of stems, seeds, and roots of the aquatic plants.

Pre-Reading Information
Strip Mining

There are many methods of mining. Which one is used depends upon where a mineral deposit is located. Strip mining is used when the desired material—coal—is located near the surface of the earth.

Strip mining involves the following steps: First, bulldozers level and clear the area. Next, explosives are set into pre-drilled holes and detonated. Then, earth-moving machines remove the unwanted soil and rock. When the desired mineral is exposed, smaller power shovels dig it up.

Strip mining digs up and destroys an enormous area of land. Serious environmental problems have been caused by this practice. Today there are federal laws requiring that after strip mining, the land must be returned, as closely as possible, to the original state.

West Virginia is the second leading coal-producing state in America.

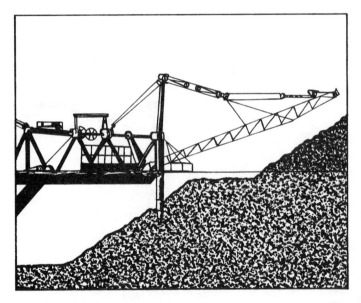

Vocabulary
Chapter One

Match the vocabulary words on the left to the definitions on the right. Place the correct letter on each line.

_____	1. abruptly	A.	puzzling; mysterious
_____	2. braced	B.	native of India; believer in Hinduism
_____	3. inscrutable	C.	square scarf often used as a headcovering
_____	4. Hindu	D.	with unexpected suddenness
_____	5. kaleidoscope	E.	to rub gently with nose or snout
_____	6. kerchief	F.	supported
_____	7. lanky	G.	expressing or arousing pity
_____	8. nuzzle	H.	awkwardly tall and thin
_____	9. pathetic	I.	instrument with mirrors and loose bits of colored glass that produces ever-changing patterns

Choose any four vocabulary words from the first part of this activity. Write an original sentence for each.

_____

_____

_____

_____

_____

_____

_____

Comprehension and Discussion Questions
Chapter One

Answer the following questions in complete sentence form. Give examples from the story to support your response.

1. Evaluate Wanda's advice to "ignore things that are wrong with you."

_____

_____

_____

_____

2. Predict what Wanda and her aunt are arguing about.

_____

_____

_____

_____

3. What were some of the things that were confusing Sara?

_____

_____

_____

4. How did Sara explain what her summer had been like? To what did she compare her life?

_____

_____

_____

_____

Vocabulary
Chapters Two and Three

Use the words and phrases in the box to complete the sentences below. You may need to use your dictionary.

crown jewel	drowsy	emphatically	fascinating	glanced
illusion	grimaced	magnesia	mechanical	pediatrician
psychology	retarded	rhododendrum	silhouette	sincerely

1. The _____ examined the sick child.

2. Although Sue was _____, she couldn't fall asleep.

3. The water appeared to be nearby, but that was only an _____.

4. Sue only _____ at the painting; therefore, she didn't recall any details.

5. Everyone listened with interest to Brendan's story; they found it _____.

6. Billy was _____; he did not learn as easily as others his age.

7. The _____ had clusters of pink flowers.

8. Mom _____ sent them to bed; her tone of voice told them she was serious.

9. Diane _____ thanked us for our help; it was obvious she meant it.

10. Pat _____ at the horrible sight; it really disgusted her.

Five of the vocabulary words were not used in the first part of this activity. Choose three of those words and write an original sentence for each.

_____

_____

_____

_____

_____

_____

Comprehension and Discussion Questions
Chapters Two and Three

Answer the following questions in complete sentence form. Give examples from the story to support your response.

1. What was bothering Charlie that caused him to shuffle his feet?

_____

_____

_____

_____

2. What was Sara's complaint about Aunt Willie?

_____

_____

_____

_____

3. Why, do you suppose, did Sara object to discussing Charlie?

_____

_____

_____

_____

4. Do you agree with Wanda that children like Charlie are everyone's problem? Explain.

_____

_____

_____

_____

Vocabulary
Chapters Four and Five

Find the following words in the fourth and fifth chapters of *The Summer of the Swans*. Use your dictionary to define the words based upon their use in the story.

earshot

flicked

hesitated

indignation

matador

muttering

piercing

pivoting

sidesaddle

spigot

staggered

strip mining

taunted

theme

uneventful

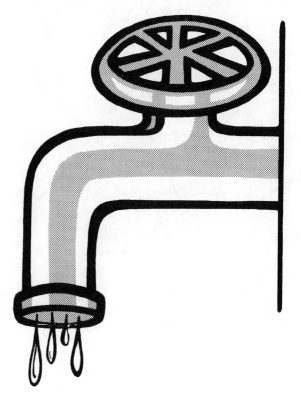

Word Webs

Using the vocabulary words that you defined in the first part of this activity, build word webs. Choose one vocabulary for each circle and write it in the center. Then fill in the blanks with words that are related to the center word. Stretch your mind! Use nouns, verbs, adverbs, etc.

An example has been done for you.

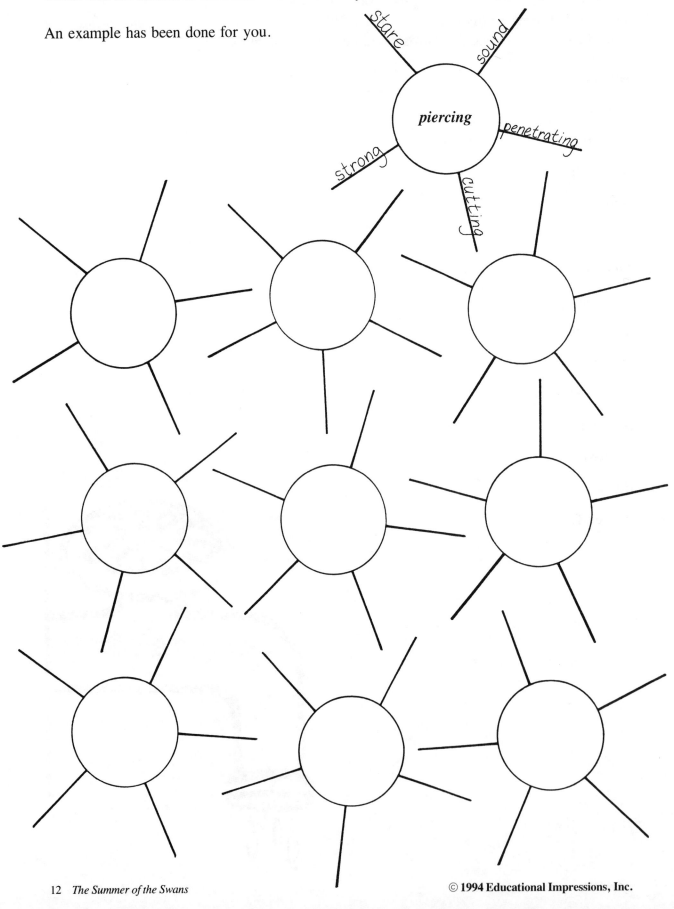

Comprehension and Discussion Questions
Chapters Four and Five

Answer the following questions in complete sentence form. Give examples from the story to support your response.

1. Explain the deal that Frank and Aunt Willie made. Judge Frank's idea.

_____

_____

_____

_____

2. Sara complained about never being able to do something. What was it that she wanted to do?

_____

_____

_____

_____

3. On a scale of one to ten, with ten being the most important, rate the importance of one's appearance from Sara's point of view. Do you agree?

_____

_____

_____

_____

4. What bothered Sara about the dress her aunt had made for her?

_____

_____

_____

_____

Vocabulary
Chapters Six and Seven

For each sentence circle the most appropriate definition for the word printed in bold as it is used in the sentence. Use your dictionary to help you. The first has been done for you.

1. The crowd was **clamoring** for attention.

    crying out   waving wildly   singing loudly

2. Meg was **content** to sit quietly and listen to the birds.

   topics   annoyed   satisfied

3. One of the wagon wheels was stuck in the **ditch**.

   discard   trench   forced landing

4. The **elegance** of the bride's dress was noted by all.

   tasteful richness   fabric   color

5. Mark's story was **incredible.**

   phony   unbelievable   funny

6. The boys **impatiently** waited for the rain to stop.

   angrily   restlessly   quietly

7. Andrew **snatched** the book from Billy.

   grabbed   stole   borrowed

8. Tiger's paw was **wedged** into the crack in the wall.

   jammed   pie-shaped   pointed

9. The vines **tugged** at the pine tree.

   banged   looked   pulled

Comprehension and Discussion Questions
Chapters Six and Seven

Answer the following questions in complete sentence form. Give examples from the story to support your response.

1. What worked like a magic charm for Charlie?

_____

_____

_____

_____

2. How did Sara get Charlie to agree to leave the swans?

_____

_____

_____

_____

3. Sara realized that she was unhappy with herself and her family. She had not felt this way before. Try to explain this change.

_____

_____

_____

_____

4. Judge Sara's treatment of Charlie in these chapters.

_____

_____

_____

_____

Vocabulary
Chapters Eight and Nine

Alphabetize the words in the box. Then find the words (or forms of the words) in chapters eight and nine of the book. Use your dictionary to define them as they were used in the story.

stumble	affected	banister	blaring	whine
monitor	gauze	vacant	gross	persist
tremble	shuffle	splendor	dedication	thump
puce	linoleum	tormented	hobbling	gullies

Choose four of the words and write an original sentence for each.

_____

_____

_____

_____

_____

_____

Comprehension and Discussion Questions
Chapter Eight

Answer the following questions in complete sentence form. Give examples from the story to support your response.

1. What were Sara's reasons for not liking Frank?

_____

_____

_____

_____

2. How would you describe Sara and Wanda's relationship? Give evidence to support your opinion.

_____

_____

_____

_____

3. What was keeping Sara awake?

_____

_____

_____

_____

4. What was the cause of Charlie's mental problem?

_____

_____

_____

_____

Comprehension and Discussion Questions
Chapter Nine

Answer the following questions in complete sentence form. Give examples from the story to support your response.

1. What was making Charlie restless and keeping him from sleeping?

_____

_____

_____

_____

2. What two colors mixed to result in the puce tennis shoes? Describe the color puce.

_____

_____

_____

_____

3. How did Charlie interpret the rule about never leaving the yard?

_____

_____

_____

_____

4. Where was Charlie going? Why?

_____

_____

_____

_____

Vocabulary
Chapters Ten and Eleven

Define the words in the box. You may need to use your dictionary.

awkwardness	briers	frayed	gasping	maze
rasping	scanned	startle	soothing	thrashed
chide	discouraged	pomegranante	Pomeranian	posse

Word Categories

After you have discovered the meanings of the vocabulary words, place them into as many different categories as possible. You must have at least two words to a group. Give each category a title. You may use a word in more than one category. Two examples have been started for you. Have fun!

SOUNDS

rasping
gasping

SIX-LETTER WORDS

briers
frayed

Comprehension and Discussion Questions
Chapters Ten and Eleven

Answer the following questions in complete sentence form. Give examples from the story to support your response.

1. What caused Charlie to feel afraid and become confused?

_____

_____

_____

_____

2. As Charlie went deeper into the forest, a feeling overcame him. Describe that feeling.

_____

_____

_____

_____

3. How was Charlie's disappearance discovered?

_____

_____

_____

_____

4. Why wasn't Sara very worried until she reached the lake?

_____

_____

_____

_____

Vocabulary
Chapter Twelve

Match the vocabulary words on the left to the definitions on the right. Place the correct letter on each line.

_____ 1. agitation

A. payment demanded for release

_____ 2. befallen

B. returning evil for evil

_____ 3. elongated

C. deep, narrow gorge

_____ 4. grudgingly

D. sorrowfully; with an expression of grief

_____ 5. mournfully

E. disappeared

_____ 6. revenge

F. disastrous events

_____ 7. ravine

G. emotional disturbance

_____ 8. vanished

H. lengthened; extended

_____ 9. tragedies

I. unwillingly; with resentment

_____ 10. ransom

J. happened to

You Are There!

Pretend that you are a reporter for the *West Virginia Herald*. Describe Charlie's disappearance. Use six or more vocabulary words from the first part of this activity in your story.

Comprehension and Discussion Questions
Chapter Twelve

Answer the following questions in complete sentence form. Give examples from the story to support your response.

1. Why did Sara say, "Aunt Willie, don't call yet. Maybe—"? Do you think Aunt Willie made the right decision when she called the police? Explain.

_____

_____

_____

_____

2. Why did Aunt Willie refer to the television as "that devil television"?

_____

_____

_____

_____

3. Give two examples of how Sara took revenge against people she thought had ridiculed her brother.

_____

_____

_____

_____

4. According to Aunt Willie, in what way did Sara take after her Uncle Bert? Judge Sara's actions. Do you think that revenge is always warranted?

_____

_____

_____

_____

Vocabulary
Chapter Thirteen

Define the following words based upon their use in the story. You may have to use your dictionary.

1. **absorb**

2. **adoring**

3. **bonded**

4. **disrespectful**

5. **occasional**

6. **remote**

7. **skinned**

8. **sober**

9. **sustain**

Lost!

Have you ever been lost? Have you known a close friend or relative who has been lost? How did you (or your friend or relative) feel? What actions did you (or your friend or relative) take? Tell about the experience in a well written story. If neither you nor anyone close to you has had this experience, imagine what it would feel like to be lost and by yourself. Use at least four or more vocabulary words from the first part of this activity in your story.

Comprehension and Discussion Questions
Chapter Thirteen

Answer the following questions in complete sentence form. Give examples from the story to support your response.

1. Why was Sara reluctant to let Aunt Willie call her father and ask him to come?

_____

_____

_____

_____

2. What caused Sara's father to become estranged from the family? Judge his reasons.

_____

_____

_____

_____

3. Why, do you think, did Aunt Willie put on her best dress?

_____

_____

_____

_____

4. How did Aunt Willie's opinion of Sara's father differ from Sara's opinion of him? Why, do you think, was this the case?

_____

_____

_____

_____

Vocabulary
Chapters Fourteen and Fifteen

Use the following words in original sentences that clearly show the meanings of the words. You may need to use your dictionary.

1. **accusation:** _____

_____

2. **casually:** _____

_____

3. **exaggerate:** _____

_____

4. **fiercely:** _____

_____

5. **hustled:** _____

_____

6. **incident:** _____

_____

7. **immediately:** _____

_____

8. **particular:** _____

_____

9. **transistor:** _____

_____

10. **triumph:** _____

_____

Word Search

Use the words from the first part of this activity to make a Word Search Puzzle in the grid.

accusation   casually   exaggerate

fiercely   hustled   incident   immediately

particular   transistor   triumph

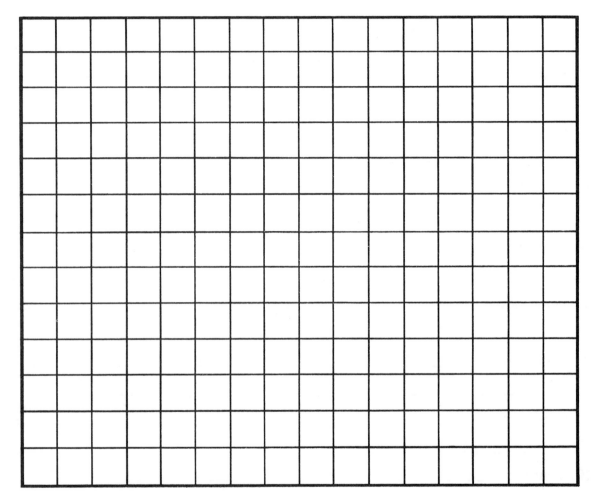

Comprehension and Discussion Questions
Chapters Fourteen and Fifteen

Answer the following questions in complete sentence form. Give examples from the story to support your response.

1. What caused tears to come to Sara's eyes?

_____

_____

_____

_____

2. Who were the real culprits in the watch incident?

_____

_____

_____

_____

3. Do you agree with Sara that Aunt Willie did a terrible thing by going to see Joe's mother? Explain your point of view.

_____

_____

_____

_____

4. Have you ever made a false accusation and regretted it later? Tell about your experience. How did you feel when you learned the truth?

_____

_____

_____

_____

Vocabulary
Chapter Sixteen

Use the words and phrases in the box to complete the sentences below. You may need to use your dictionary.

profile	**associates**	**interrupted**	**impetuous**
crudely	**desperate**	**nauseated**	**indestructible**
prowling	**cicadas**	**hastily**	**criticism**

1. She _____ the color blue with peacefulness.

2. The male _____ make a shrill sound during the hot, dry weather.

3. The thief was caught _____ around the jewelry store.

4. The reviewer wrote a sharp _____ of the new play.

5. Dave's quick purchase of a new car seemed like an _____ act.

6. The strong fortress was said to be _____.

7. The artist painted the little girl in _____, not in full face.

8. They were _____ for a drink of water after crossing the desert.

9. When the ship began to rock, the some of the passengers became _____.

10. They found a hut that was _____ made of mud and straw.

11. An announcer _____ the scheduled program to give an urgent report.

12. They _____ made a decision, but they later regretted it.

I'm Innocent!

From Joe's point of view, summarize the watch incident. How did you feel when confronted by Aunt Willie? How did you feel when Sara told you that she thought you were guilty? How do you feel now that Sara has apologized? Use at least five of the vocabulary words from the first part of this activity.

Comprehension and Discussion Questions
Chapter Sixteen

Answer the following questions in complete sentence form. Give examples from the story to support your response.

1. Why was Sara so sure that Charlie would not enter the mine?

_____

_____

_____

_____

2. What caused Sara to become annoyed at Mary? How would you have felt in this situation if you had been Sara?

_____

_____

_____

_____

3. Sara thought that she understood how Charlie felt about things. How did she try to prove her point?

_____

_____

_____

_____

4. Characterize Joe. Describe the qualities that might have made him a good companion for Sara.

_____

_____

_____

_____

Vocabulary
Chapters Seventeen, Eighteen, and Nineteen

Read each clue and find the answers in the box. Then use the letters above the numbered spaces to decipher the secret message. Some of the words will not be used.

flail	outstretched	engulf	finality	clammy
intersection	foliage	compulsion	betray	anguish
cascade	dialogue	roused	dullness	tremulous

1. be disloyal
    — — — — —
    ⁴

2. small waterfall
    — — — — — —
    ³   ⁷

3. extended
    — — — — — — — — — — —
              ¹ ²

4. thrash around
    — — — —
    ⁶ ⁵

5. leaves of a plant
    — — — — — —
        ⁸

6. impulse that is hard to resist
    — — — — — — — —
          ¹² ⁹

7. the end; state of being final
    — — — — — — —
    ¹⁰

8. meeting of roads
    — — — — — — — — — — — —
                  ¹¹

9. overwhelm; swallow up
    — — — — — —
      ¹³

10. conversation
    — — — — — — — —
    ¹⁴

1 2 3 4 5 6 7   8 9   10 11 12 13 14

— — — — — — —   — —   — — — — —

Comprehension and Discussion Questions
Chapters Seventeen, Eighteen, and Nineteen

Answer the following questions in complete sentence form. Give examples from the story to support your response.

1. What made Charlie suddenly seem to explode inside?

_____

_____

_____

_____

2. What made Sara feel a little better?

_____

_____

_____

_____

3. Joe tried to encourage Sara by saying, "Keep coming. We're almost there." To what did Sara compare this statement?

_____

_____

_____

_____

4. Why did Sara say, "When I have a true sadness, there are no tears left"? What lesson do you think Sara was learning?

_____

_____

_____

_____

Vocabulary
Chapters Twenty and Twenty-one

Find the following words in chapters twenty and twenty-one. Define the words according to their use in the story. You may need to use your dictionary.

1. **absolutely:** _____

2. **clasp:** _____

3. **clenched:** _____

4. **dread:** _____

5. **frenzy:** _____

6. **glittering:** _____

7. **grasp:** _____

8. **heaving:** _____

9. **knickknacks:** _____

10. **procedure:** _____

11. **quick:** _____

12. **topple:** _____

13. **twitched:** _____

14. **unspent:** _____

Synonyms

A synonym is a word that has a meaning similar to that of another word. Choose eight words from the first part of this activity. Write a synonym for each.

© **1994 Educational Impressions, Inc.**

Comprehension and Discussion Questions
Chapters Twenty and Twenty-one

Answer the following questions in complete sentence form. Give examples from the story to support your response.

1. Why was a structured life so important to Charlie?

_____

_____

_____

_____

2. How did Charlie react to the sound of someone calling his name? What was Sara's response to Charlie's cries?

_____

_____

_____

_____

3. From Sara's point of view, describe the discovery of Charlie.

_____

_____

_____

_____

4. Joe helped to comfort Charlie. Explain how he accomplished this.

_____

_____

_____

_____

Vocabulary
Chapters Twenty-two and Twenty-three

Choose the word in each set that is **most like** the first word in meaning.

1. **amplifier:**   stereo   loudspeaker   radio

2. **urgent:**   deliberate   soon   pressing

3. **pasture:**   grassland   swamp   park

4. **associate:**   assist   connect   business

5. **beacon:**   signal   food   building

6. **enormous:**   wide   huge   elastic

7. **occasionally:**   once   never   sometimes

8. **mute:**   noisy   scared   voiceless

9. **shrill:**   piercing   low   noisy

10. **jamming:**   crowding   painting   sketching

Making Conversation

Create a dialogue between two story characters. For example, what might Sara say to her father when she finally sees him. How might he respond to her? Use at least six vocabulary words from the first part of this activity in your creative conversation.

Comprehension and Discussion Questions
Chapters Twenty-two and Twenty-three

Answer the following questions in complete sentence form. Give examples from the story to support your response.

1. Analyze the reasons Sara suddenly felt good.

_____

_____

_____

_____

2. Why did Sara hesitate before responding to Joe's invitation?

_____

_____

_____

_____

3. Why was Wanda angry? Was she justified? Explain.

_____

_____

_____

_____

4. Sara compared life to a series of steps. According to her, how did the ways in which she and her father confronted those steps differ? How do you confront the steps in your life?

_____

_____

_____

_____

Spotlight Literary Skill
Characterization

Characterization is the method used by an author to give readers information about a character. The author tries to show the character's strengths, weaknesses, and other qualities. In *The Summer of the Swans,* Charlie gets lost and is reported missing! Please fill out this Missing Person's Report in order to help authorities locate him.

MISSING PERSON POLICE REPORT

CHARACTER PROFILE

Name of Missing Person:

Age:

Last Known Address:

Physical Description:

Personality Traits:

Family Information (Names, Descriptions, and Whereabouts):

Cause of Disappearance:

Special Problems:

Possible Whereabouts:

MUG SHOT
(Sketch a Picture of the Missing Person)

Other Pertinent Information:

Spotlight Literary Skill
Plot

A **plot** is a sequence of events that tells a story. You have just read *The Summer of the Swans*. Put the following story events in the order as they occurred in the plot. Number the events from 1 to 15. Then rewrite the sentences in their proper order.

_____ Aunt Willie calls the children's father.

_____ Sara passes Joe Melby at the baseball field, and he offers to help look for Charlie.

_____ Sara slides down the bank to Charlie.

_____ Charlie's watch stops.

_____ Aunt Willie goes for a ride on Frank's motor scooter.

_____ Sara dyes her tennis shoes.

_____ Joe shows Sara and Mary the brown slipper.

_____ Sara takes Charlie to the lake to see the swans.

_____ Mary goes with Sara to the lake.

_____ Sara takes her toast and goes onto the front porch.

_____ Sara and Joe climb to the top of the hill and look out at the valley.

_____ Sara apologizes to Joe.

_____ Joe lends Charlie his watch.

_____ Joe invites Sara to Benny's party.

_____ Charlie cries out in a hoarse, excited voice.

Spotlight Literary Skill
Dialogue

Dialogue, the spoken words of the characters, is an important feature of many types of writing. In this story the characters seem to come alive when we hear them speak to each other. Through the dialogue, we learn more about how each character thinks, feels, and relates to others. The use of dialogue allows the readers to feel present at the scene of the action.

There are many excellent examples of realistic dialogue in this novel. Write five of your favorites. For each, explain the circumstances.

1.

2.

3.

4.

5.

At the Party!

Betsy Byars did not describe what happened when Sara went to the party with Joe. In the space below, create a dialogue that might have taken place between two of the story characters who were at the party.

Spotlight Literary Skill
Symbolism

A **symbol** is something that stands for a larger or more complex object or idea. Often, it is the use of a concrete thing to represent an idea or concept that cannot itself be shown visually. For example, the American flag, Uncle Sam, and the Statue of Liberty are all symbols of a nation, the United States of America.

In literature, **symbolism** is the use of a thing, character, object, or idea to represent something else. In *The Summer of the Swans,* Charlie delighted in visiting the swans at the lake. The swans, however, were symbolic of a more important idea in the story. Can you explain this idea? Give examples from the story to back up your reasoning.

Cooperative Learning Activity
Changes

How did Sara's feelings about each of the following characters change during the course of the story? Give specific examples or quotes from the story to support your opinion.

CHARACTER	Beginning	End
Wanda		
Joe Melby		
Father		
Charlie		
Herself		

Add your ideas as you read the book. Then share your answers with members of your Cooperative Learning Group. Finally, compare your group's ideas with those of other classroom groups.

Post-Reading Activity
Critic's Corner

Pretend that you are writing a review of *The Summer of the Swans* for the Book Review section of your daily newspaper. Your job is to provide information about the book and to evaluate its worth for your readers. Be sure to include the setting, plot, and characterization as well as your general opinion. Among the topics you may want to discuss are the believability of the plot and characters, the appropriateness of the vocabulary, and the writing style of the author.

The Summer of the Swans

_____

_____

_____

_____

_____

_____

_____

_____

_____

_____

_____

_____

_____

_____

_____

_____

_____

_____

_____

Post-Reading Activity
Create-A-Sequel

Create a sequel to this story. Think about the following questions before you begin:

What happens to the main characters in future years?

Is Sara able to maintain her improved self-image?

Does Wanda continue her relationship with Frank?

Is Charlie ever able to lead an independent life?

Does the children's relationship with their father change?

_____

_____

_____

_____

_____

_____

_____

_____

_____

_____

_____

_____

_____

_____

_____

_____

Give your new story a title. Share your story with your classmates.

More Post-Reading Activities

1. Research various forms of mental retardation. Locate local agencies that provide services for the mentally retarded and describe these programs to the class. How can you best help schoolmates, family members, and/or friends who have this condition?

2. Think about the lessons you have learned from reading this story. Describe these lessons and tell how they can be applied to your daily life.

3. Pretend that you are in Sara's position. What would you do differently to solve your problems?

4. Create an attractive book jacket that captures the theme of the story.

5. Write a story about a character who becomes a winner after struggling against some kind of handicap or special problem. Give your story an interesting title.

Glossary of Literary Terms

Alliteration: A repetition of initial, or beginning, sounds in two or more consecutive or neighboring words.

Analogy: A comparison based upon the resemblance in some particular ways between things that are otherwise unlike.

Anecdote: A short account of an interesting, amusing, or biographical occurrence.

Anticlimax: An event that is less important than what occurred before it.

Archaic language: Language that was once common in a particular historic period but which is no longer commonly used.

Cause and effect: The relationship in which one condition brings about another condition as a direct result. The result, or consequence, is called the effect.

Character development: The ways in which the author shows how a character changes as the story proceeds.

Characterization: The method used by the author to give readers information about a character; a description or representation of a person's qualities or peculiarities.

Classify: To arrange according to a category or trait.

Climax: The moment when the action in a story reaches its greatest conflict.

Compare and contrast: To examine the likenesses and differences of two people, ideas, or things. (*Contrast* always emphasizes differences. *Compare* may focus on likenesses alone or on likenesses and differences.)

Conflict: The main source of drama and tension in a literary work; the discord between persons or forces that brings about dramatic action.

Connotation: Something suggested or implied, not actually stated.

Description: An account that gives the reader a mental image or picture of something.

Dialect: A form of language used in a certain geographic region; it is distinguished from the standard form of the language by pronunciation, grammar, and/or vocabulary.

Dialogue (dialog): The parts of a literary work that represent conversation.

Fact: A piece of information that can be proven or verified.

Figurative language: Description of one thing in terms usually used for something else. Simile and metaphor are examples of figurative language.

Flashback: The insertion of an earlier event into the normal chronological sequence of a narrative.

Foreshadowing: The use of clues to give readers a hint of events that will occur later on.

Historical fiction: Fiction represented in a setting true to the history of the time in which the story takes place.

Imagery: Language that appeals to the senses; the use of figures of speech or vivid descriptions to produce mental images.

Irony: The use of words to express the opposite of their literal meaning.

Legend: A story handed down from earlier times; its truth is popularly accepted but cannot be verified.

Limerick: A humorous five-lined poem with a specific form: aabba. Lines 1, 2, and 5 are longer than lines 3 and 4.

Metaphor: A figure of speech that compares two unlike things without the use of like or as.

Mood: The feeling that the author creates for the reader.

Motivation: The reasons for the behavior of a character.

Narrative: The type of writing that tells a story.

Narrator: The character who tells the story.

Opinion: A personal point of view or belief.

Parody: Writing that ridicules or imitates something more serious.

Personification: A figure of speech in which an inanimate object or an abstract idea is given human characteristics.

Play: A literary work that is written in dialogue form and that is usually performed before an audience.

Plot: The arrangement or sequence of events in a story.

Point of view: The perspective from which a story is told.

Protagonist: The main character.

Pun: A play on words that are similar in sound but different in meaning.

Realistic fiction: True-to-life fiction; the people, places, and happenings are similar to those in real life.

Resolution: The part of the plot from the climax to the ending where the main dramatic conflict is worked out.

Satire: A literary work that pokes fun at individual or societal weaknesses.

Sequencing: The placement of story elements in the order of their occurrence.

Setting: The time and place in which the story occurs.

Simile: A figure of speech that uses *like* or *as* to compare two unlike things.

Stereotype: A character whose personality traits represent a group rather than an individual.

Suspense: Quality that causes readers to wonder what will happen next.

Symbolism: The use of a thing, character, object, or idea to represent something else.

Synonyms: Words that are very similar in meaning.

Tall tale: An exaggerated story detailing unbelievable events.

Theme: The main idea of a literary work; the message the author wants to communicate, sometimes expressed as a generalization about life.

Tone: The quality or feeling conveyed by the work; the author's style or manner of expression.

ANSWERS

Chapter One: Vocabulary

1. D	3. A	5. I	7. H	9. G
2. F	4. B	6. C	8. E	

Chapter One: Comprehension and Discussion Questions (Answers may vary.)

1. Answers will vary.

2. Answers will vary, but some might guess that it had something to do with going out with Frank.

3. The same things that were making her unhappy this summer did not make her unhappy last summer. She compared her life to a kaleidoscope. The elements were the same, but the results were different.

4. She said that her summer had been like a seesaw, filled with ups and downs and out of her control.

Chapters Two and Three: Vocabulary

1. pediatrician	3. illusion	5. fascinating	7. rhododendron	9. sincerely
2. drowsy	4. glanced	6. retarded	8. emphatically	10. grimaced

Chapters Two and Three: Comprehension and Discussion Questions (Answers may vary.)

1. He had separated the candy from the stick and was afraid that Sara would take the candy from him as she had threatened to do.

2. Sara didn't like the way she bossed them around, didn't really listen to what they said, and embarrassed them by telling personal things to others.

3. Sara felt that Charlie was their problem and no one else's. She may have been embarrassed by his condition.

4. Answers will vary.

Chapters Four and Five: Comprehension and Discussion Questions (Answers may vary.)

1. Aunt Willie would take a ride with Frank on the scooter. If she still objected after the ride, Wanda wouldn't go on the scooter.

2. Sara complained that she never got to do anything by herself. During the day she had to watch over Charlie and at night she had to share a room with Wanda.

3. Sara would rank it a 10. ''I think how you look is the most important thing in the world.''

4. Her aunt had promised that the stripes would meet, but they didn't.

Chapters Six and Seven: Vocabulary

1. crying out	3. trench	5. unbelievable	7. grabbed	9. pulled
2. satisfied	4. tasteful richness	6. restlessly	8. jammed	

Chapters Six and Seven: Comprehension and Discussion Questions (Answers may vary.)

1. There was something about the rhythmic ticking of the watch that soothed and calmed him. It blocked out the rest of the world.

2. Sara used the watch. She showed him the spot on the watch that represented five more minutes, and he agreed to leave then.

3. Answers will vary, but many will realize that adolescence—the period between childhood and adulthood—is often a time of confusion.

4. Answers will vary. She kept him waiting at Mary's house and she also hurried him away from the swans; nevertheless, she did take him with her to see the swans.

Chapter Eight: Comprehension and Discussion Questions (Answers may vary.)

1. Sara objected to the fact that he didn't pay attention to Charlie. Also, she thought he was affected and pretentious in the way he called Wanda by pet names. Probably, she didn't really dislike him at all.

2. They seem to have had a close relationship. Sara confided in Wanda. Wanda was understanding; when she saw that Sara was upset, she stopped teasing her.

3. Although there were other noises, the restless sounds coming from Charlie's room bothered her the most. His faint kicking of the wall over and over again especially disturbed her.

4. When Charlie was three, he had had two near-fatal illnesses, each with high fevers. Although he recovered, he was left brain damaged.

Chapter Nine: Comprehension and Discussion Questions (Answers may vary.)

1. He was upset about a button that was missing from his pajamas.

2. Orange and blue mixed together. Puce is a brownish purple.

3. He associated the rule with the noisy traffic and other goings-on of the daytime. The things that usually confused him most were gone. The silence and soft darkness were reassuring.

4. Charlie was going to the lake to see the swans again. He thought that he had seen one of the swans and he couldn't get the swans out of his head.

Chapters Ten and Eleven: Comprehension and Discussion Questions (Answers may vary.)

1. He could not see anything familiar. The sound of the barking dogs frightened him; the dogs seemed to be everywhere. He didn't know which way to run.

2. There were unfamiliar smells and noises. He was overcome by a feeling of hopelessness because he thought that he would never again see his home.

3. Aunt Willie asked Sara to get Charlie and to come for breakfast. Sara searched the house, porch, and tent for Charlie, but she couldn't find him.

4. She had been sure that he would be at the lake.

Chapter Twelve: Vocabulary

1. G	3. H	5. D	7. C	9. F
2. J	4. I	6. B	8. E	10. A

Chapter Twelve: Comprehension and Discussion Questions (Answers may vary.)

1. If they called the police, it would make it seem final—as if they were admitting that he was really lost. She was not ready to face reality and thought that she could find him herself. Also, she may have been embarrassed by the idea of having the police come to her home.

2. Aunt Willie felt guilty because she had been more interested in watching a TV show than in helping Charlie with his button. She thought that perhaps she was somehow to blame for his running away.

3. She wet Gretchen Wyant's silk dress with a hose. She wrote FINK on a sign and put it on Joe Melby's back.

4. She said that Sara—like her uncle—held a grudge and never let bygones by bygones.

Chapter Thirteen: Comprehension and Discussion Questions (Answers may vary.)

1. Sara's father did not have a close or warm relationship with the children. Sara resented his remoteness. She did not believe that he would come.

2. He could not deal with the tragedy of Charlie's illness and his wife's death.

3. She probably put it on because the police would be coming to her home and she wanted to look presentable.

4. Sara resented her father; she felt that he had deserted her. Aunt Willie did not feel deserted by him. In fact, her feelings were quite opposite. He had cared for her and her family after the death of their father. She respected him for having raised two families (although Sara probably felt that he had given up raising the second).

Chapters Fourteen and Fifteen: Comprehension and Discussion Questions (Answers may vary.)

1. It was probably a combination of things: She realized that she may have been wrong about Joe. She felt awkward. She may have felt touched—but at the same time embarrassed—by the boys' desire to help. She was very worried about Charlie.

2. The boys standing outside the store had taken the watch to tease Charlie. Joe had not been one of them.

3. Answers will vary.

4. Answers will vary.

Chapter Sixteen: Vocabulary

1. associates	3. prowling	5. impetuous	7. profile	9. nauseated	11. interrupted
2. cicadas	4. criticism	6. indestructible	8. desperate	10. crudely	12. hastily

Charlie is found.

Chapter Sixteen: Comprehension and Discussion Questions (Answers may vary.)

1. Charlie was afraid of cold, dark places. He wouldn't even go into the Bryants' cellar.

2. Mary kept talking about going to Bennie Hoffman's party. Sara thought that she was bragging and also that she wasn't really interested in finding Charlie. Also, Sara was probably jealous that she hadn't been invited.

3. One day, when Sara was contemplating the vastness of the sky and trying to understand how it went on forever, she became very frustrated—almost to the point of feeling ill. She realized that that was how Charlie probably felt about everything, including most things that others understand easily and take for granted.

4. Joe was helpful, forgiving, understanding, compassionate, and friendly. He was willing to help even when he knew Sara was accusing him wrongly.

Chapters Seventeen, Eighteen, and Nineteen: Vocabulary

1. betray	3. outstretched	5. foliage	7. finality	9. engulf
2. cascade	4. flail	6. compulsion	8. intersection	10. dialogue

Chapters Seventeen, Eighteen, and Nineteen: Comprehension and Discussion Questions (Answers may vary.)

1. He was very upset at having broken his watch. When the chipmunk disappeared, it was the last straw. The situation was more than he could take.

2. She was hopeful that she would be able to see Charlie from the top of the hill.

3. She compared it to the dentist telling her that he was almost finished drilling and then drilling more.

4. All summer she had been crying over trivial matters. Now that she really had something important to be upset about, she could not cry. Answers may vary, but should include the fact that she seemed to be getting her priorities in order and learning the difference between the superficial and what really matters.

Chapters Twenty and Twenty-one: Comprehension and Discussion Questions (Answers may vary.)

1. He had gotten used to certain things. As long as this routine was kept up, he felt safe. If there were changes, he got upset and could not deal with them.

2. He cried out in a hoarse, excited voice and began to scream. When Sara realized it was Charlie, she jumped up and down. Then she sat down and scooted down the bank. She then ran down the hill until she had to stop and catch her breath. She walked along the edge of the ravine until she saw him.

3. Answers will vary, but should include that she was greatly relieved.

4. Joe gave Charlie his own watch to wear.

Chapters Twenty-two and Twenty-three: Vocabulary

1. loudspeaker	3. grassland	5. signal	7. sometimes	9. piercing
2. pressing	4. connect	6. huge	8. voiceless	10. crowding

Chapters Twenty-two and Twenty-three: Comprehension and Discussion Questions (Answers may vary.)

1. Charlie had been found. Sara realized that she had a good friend in Joe. She felt good about herself. She was beginning to learn how to overlook the little things that had bothered her before.

2. She was afraid that the invitation wasn't genuine. She thought that she might have heard wrong or that it might have been meant for someone else.

3. She was angry because no one had told her about Charlie's disappearance; she heard it on the radio without being forewarned.

4. Her father just sat at the bottom of the steps; he had given up trying to climb them. She had just taken an enormous step and was ready to face the other steps yet to come.

Spotlight Literary Skill: Sequencing

The sentences should be ordered in the following manner: 5, 7, 13, 10, 1, 3, 8, 2, 4, 6, 11, 9, 14, 15, and 12.

Spotlight Literary Skill: Symbolism

The ugly duckling who turns into a beautiful swan is symbolic of Sara, who turned into a "beautiful swan" after going through some "growing pains." At the start of the story she disliked herself, thought herself ugly, and envied her beautiful sister. "She was filled with a discontent, an anger about herself, her life, her family, that made her think she would never be content again." At the end of the story, after finding Charlie, realizing that Joe was her friend, and understanding her father a bit more, Sara no longer felt restless. She had become confident about herself and about her future. The swan also symbolized a kind of freedom for Sara. Swans are creatures who can change places easily. Sara had wanted to fly away from everything, like the swans flying to a new lake. At the end of the story, however, Sara did not feel that way anymore. She was happy to be Sara.

Cooperative Learning Activity: Changes

Wanda: In the beginning she was envious of her beautiful oler sister. "We are so different. Wanda is a hundred times prettier than I." At the end she was more self-confident. She did not seem to be envious.

Joe: In the beginning she disliked Joe and was unable to admit she could be wrong about him. In the end she admitted that "a person can occasionally be mistaken." "He is not my enemy, Wanda. He is one of the nicest people I know."

Father: In the beginning, Sara could not even listen to her aunt's conversation with her father. In the end, she seemed to be more understanding. She remembered the good times before her mother's death and her brother's illness.

Charlie: She seemed somewhat impatient with him. Although she clearly loved him, she resented having to spend so much time with him. At the end she appreciated how much he meant to her.

Herself: In the beginning she felt ugly and was highly critical of herself. At the end, she felt happy with herself. She was more self-confident. "She had just taken an enormous step...and there were other steps in front of her, so that she could go as high as the sky." Although her feet were dyed blue, she didn't dwell on this fact and got ready for the party.